Spooky!

MICHAELA MORGAN

Illustrated by Stephen Lewis

OXFORD
UNIVERSITY PRESS

OXFORD

UNIVERSITY PRESS

Great Clarendon Street, Oxford OX2 6DP

Oxford University Press is a department of the University of Oxford.
It furthers the University's objective of excellence in research, scholarship,
and education by publishing worldwide in

Oxford   New York

Auckland   Cape Town   Dar es Salaam   Hong Kong   Karachi
Kuala Lumpur   Madrid   Melbourne   Mexico City   Nairobi
New Delhi   Shanghai   Taipei   Toronto

With offices in

Argentina   Austria   Brazil   Chile   Czech Republic   France   Greece
Guatemala   Hungary   Italy   Japan   Poland   Portugal   Singapore
South Korea   Switzerland   Thailand   Turkey   Ukraine   Vietnam

Oxford is a registered trade mark of Oxford University Press
in the UK and in certain other countries

British Library Cataloguing in Publication Data
Data available

ISBN-13: 978-0-19-918389-0
ISBN-10: 0-19-918389-9

3 5 7 9 10 8 6 4 2

Available in packs
Stage 13 More Stories A Pack of 6:
ISBN-13: 978-0-19-918386-9; ISBN-10: 0-19-918386-4
Stage 13 More Stories A Class Pack:
ISBN-13: 978-0-19-918393-7; ISBN-10: 0-19-918393-7
Guided Reading Cards also available:
ISBN-13: 978-0-19-918395-1; ISBN-10: 0-19-918395-3

Cover artwork by Stephen Lewis
Photograph of Michaela Morgan © Richard Drewe

Printed in China by Imago

*Thanks to Hannah Ellison, who on a writing course in Room One in the
ancient mill, in a sudden storm, wrote the rough draft of the poem
which is included on page 25.*

1

Haunted house?

The minibus pulled to a stop. Thirteen children rushed to see where they were going to stay. 'Don't run!' shouted Miss Jackson, the teacher.

Then she stopped. Everyone stared at the house in front of them.

Everyone went quiet.

'Wow!' said Martin at last.

'It's so... big!' said Alice.

'It's so... so... spooky!' said Katie and she shivered.

The children had come for a weekend course.

Katie had been looking forward to this trip for ages.

She had spent days feeling excited
and nervous at the same time. She felt
even more nervous now she'd seen the
house they were going to stay in.

'I've never seen a house as old as this!'
said Martin.

The door opened with a creak. 'Come in. Come in,' said a deep voice.

The rest of the children will be arriving soon.

Miss Jackson and the children went in and they dumped their bags in the hall.

They looked around them at the wooden walls, the cobwebby ceilings and the rickety old staircase.

'I thought this was supposed to be a youth hostel!' said Martin. 'It looks more like a museum.'

But even Martin went quiet when he felt the chill in the air.

'Why's it so cold in here?' he said.

'It's always chilly here,' said the man who had let them in. 'It's because of the gho...'

'That's enough of that, Joe,' a thin woman interrupted. 'I won't have you scaring these children before they've even settled in.'

2

The tapestry

'I'm Marge,' said the woman. 'This is
Joe. We look after this youth hostel.
While we're waiting for the others to
arrive I'll show you around the place.'

'As you can see,' said Marge, 'this is a
very ancient building. It's five hundred
years old. Once it was a mill. Malt was
stored here, but that was long ago.'

Marge led them upstairs to show them to their rooms. She stopped on the stairs, turned to the children and spoke.

You are now looking at one of the oldest things in the house.

Martin giggled.

'Not me, silly,' smiled Marge. 'This tapestry. A tapestry is a picture – but not a picture that's been painted. It's a picture that has been sewn – or woven. This one is as old as the house and it shows life as it used to be here.'

The children crowded round. 'Don't touch it!' warned Marge. 'It's so old it might crumble!'

'Like the rest of the house,' said Martin. But really he was just as impressed as all the other children.

The tapestry was old. The colours were faded and dimmed by age.

There was a big red-faced man on a little donkey. A thin woman was running after him. She stretched her bony hand out towards him. But the fat man just laughed at her. Men were working in fields. A piper was piping and dancers were dancing.

There they all were – frozen in time.
Forever skipping stiffly. Forever singing
silently. And the thin woman forever
running behind the man on the donkey.
Forever calling to him.

But the strangest thing about the
tapestry was the smell. It smelt of damp
and dust and age… and something else.
What was it?

The children gazed at the tapestry.

'Who's the red-faced man on the donkey?' asked Alice.

'That's the miller,' said Marge. 'See, he's holding a jar of ale in his hand. We call it beer nowadays. The miller made ale with the malt from his mill. You can see that he loved his ale. But he did not love his wife. Can you see her in the tapestry?'

'Is it that thin lady who looks so sad?' asked Katie.

'Yes,' said Marge. 'And the poor lady had reason to be sad. I'll tell you her story...'

Suddenly Katie interrupted. 'What is that smell?' she asked.

'Oh, that's the smell of malt! It used to be stored here long ago,' said Marge. 'Of course we don't keep malt here any more but lots of people say they can still smell it.'

It seems to come and go with the gho...

Just then a cold wind whistled round them and a door banged. Katie shuddered.

'Someone's arrived,' said Marge. 'I'll tell you more later.'

3

The storm

The rest of the group had arrived. Katie was busy saying how spooky the house was. Martin was making everyone laugh.

'That's enough,' said their teacher.
'It's time for our first evening session.
We'll use Room One right at the top of
the house.'

The children clattered up the wooden stairs to Room One. It was a huge room with high ceilings and beams across the roof space.

Above them, on the roof, pigeons scuttled and cooed. Through the tiny old window you could glimpse the street below them. Darkness was falling.

Their teacher gave them notebooks.

'I want you to use these notebooks to record the things you see, the things you hear, think, feel and find out,' she said. 'And the first thing you're going to find out is the history of this house. I'll tell you all about it.'

'Marge started to tell us about the miller and his wife,' said Alice. 'Do you know that story?'

'Yes I do,' said Miss Jackson. 'And the story happened *here* in this very room!'

Ooh, tell us!

Everyone sat down and she began.

'This house is full of history.

'This house is full of mystery.

'This house is full of stories and here is just one of them…

'It was long, long ago in this very room. This is where the sacks of malt were stored. There used to be planks between those beams above your head. Those beams – well they could tell a story…'

But she got no further.

Suddenly the room went dark and rain lashed against the window. Lightning flashed and the wind rattled and howled at the windows.

Katie shrieked: 'Aaaaaaaaaaaaaa!'

But their teacher was excited.

All the children got excited too. They ran from window to window, writing down what they saw.

Then they listened and noted what they heard. In the gloom of that old room the atmosphere was electric. All the time the windows rattled and rain pattered against the panes as if someone was tapping, asking to come in.

What Martin wrote:

Flashes of lightning
katie thinks ~~there~~ theye frightening
Katie thinks its Spooky
But i'm not scared at all.

The windows are rattling.
katies teeth are chattering
Katie thinks its spooky
but im not scared at all
Im not afraid of stuff like that
im not a scaredy cat
Katie thinks it's spooky
but im not scared AT ALL

Katie

What Katie wrote:

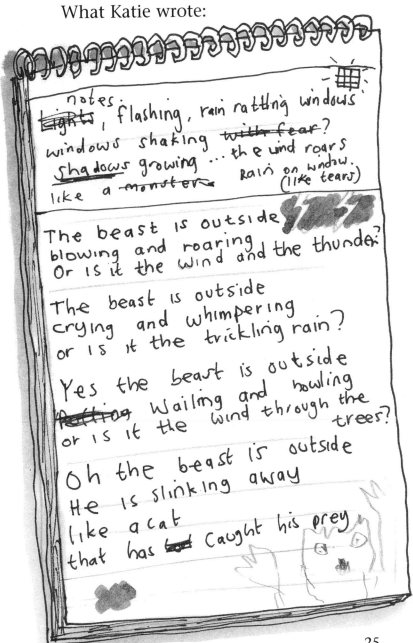

notes:
~~Light~~, flashing, rain rattling windows
windows shaking ~~with fear?~~
shadows growing ... the wind roars
like a ~~monster~~   Rain on window.
                        (like tears)

The beast is outside
blowing and roaring
Or is it the wind and the thunder?

The beast is outside
crying and whimpering
or is it the trickling rain?

Yes the beast is outside
~~rattling~~ Wailing and howling
or is it the wind through the trees?

Oh the beast is outside
He is slinking away
like a cat
that has ~~got~~ caught his prey

4

The mysterious visitor

Later, when they were all tucked up in their bunks, it seemed less exciting and more scary. Especially to Katie. She was sharing a room with Alice and Holly.

The other two had both happily giggled and chattered and then settled down for sleep.

But not Katie. She couldn't get the pictures from the tapestry out of her mind. She couldn't get the sounds of the storm out of her mind. She couldn't get the dusty sweet smell of malt out of her mind.

She was scared. Even her own poem scared her.

'What if there really is a beast outside?' she worried.

Katie lay like a stone with her sleeping bag pulled up to her chin.

In the distance she could hear the boys in their room, still whooping and laughing. In the dark their laughter sounded eerie. Bit by bit, it faded as they too gave in to sleep.

But Katie was a long way from sleep. She heard every small sound. She heard every small movement.

She missed her own bed.

She missed her old bear.

She missed her mum.

The whooshing of the traffic in the rain outside disturbed her.

The car headlights criss-crossing the ceiling made bar shapes above and around her. It was like being in a cage. Katie lay stiff and scared.

From above her there came noises – strange scratching noises and then an

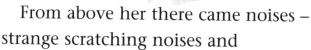

'What's that?' hissed Katie.

'Pigeons or owls,' said Alice, sleepily. 'Just go to sleep.'

But then there were the shufflings and the snufflings, the squeakings and the creakings and then a terrible gurgling sound.

'Pipes,' said Alice. 'It's just the water pipes.'

Katie closed her eyes tightly. But the gurgling seemed louder and it sounded like a monster rumbling or glugging. She opened her eyes and then she saw...

Two red eyes were shining at her.
The beast! It's the beast!

'What's that!' she whispered. But Alice
was snoring now. 'It's just the lamp post
outside,' Katie told herself.

'It looks like a monster. It sounds like
a monster. But it isn't a monster.'

There were snorings and snufflings all around her now. Someone in her room was muttering in their sleep and then... *what was that?*

Katie heard a creaking on the stairs. Someone or something was coming up. And getting closer.

She heard a padding of feet coming towards her door.

Someone or something was on the prowl.

Katie listened hard and peered at the door. Then to her horror, she saw the handle turning.

A beam of light shone into the room. Someone or something was looking around the room.

Katie held her breath till it hurt. She pulled the blanket up to her chin and peered over the top of it.

She saw a very thin woman coming towards her. Her scrawny hand was outstretched.

'The tapestry's come to life! The tapestry's come to life!' thought Katie. 'And it's coming to get me!'

A bony hand reached out towards Katie...

5

Around the fire

It was Marge.

'Are you not asleep yet, dear?' she asked. 'I'm just checking on everyone. Some of the kids in the other room have had a bit of trouble settling. So we've made a hot milky drink. Would you like to come down and have some?'

Katie sighed with relief, found her slippers and followed Marge downstairs.

There were quite a few children downstairs. They were sitting round the fire. Joe was handing round mugs of a delicious sweet-smelling drink.

'It's got that malty smell!' said one of the children.

'Yes,' said Joe. 'It's made of milk and malt. Very good for you. It's my favourite.'

One of the children was clutching a tissue. 'I've never stayed away from home before,' she sniffed.

'I know,' said Katie. 'It's strange isn't it?'

Then she noticed someone else. It couldn't be! It wouldn't be! It was! It was Martin!

'Were you spooked too?' Katie asked.

'Scared? Me! 'Course not!' he said. 'I just had a bit of trouble sleeping with all that traffic noise.'

'Yeah,' said Katie. 'Me too,' and she smiled.

6

The ghost story

The next day everything was back to
normal.

'Come on, children,' said Miss
Jackson.

It all seemed so normal in the
daylight.

Everyone had a story to tell.

Everyone had heard strange things.

'It's a very noisy old house,' said Miss Jackson. 'Everything creaks and squeaks – but that's because this is an old house. It's just old...' She looked at Katie. 'Not spooky!'

'I thought I heard a monster,' Katie admitted with a laugh.

'There is no monster here,' said their teacher, 'but some people say there is a ghost. There is no such thing as a ghost, of course, but I'll tell you the story... Is everyone here?'

Only Martin was missing. Joe had asked him to help with the washing up. So he was out of the room when they heard the whole story of the miller's wife.

Once, long ago, a miller and his wife lived here. The miller was fond of a drink. But he was not fond of hard work. His wife did all of the work.

Of course she was not happy about this – and she made sure the miller knew about her unhappiness. How she nagged him! How she complained! 'There's no end to this work,' she would say. 'I can never stop. And what do you do to help? Nothing. What are you good for? Nothing!'

For years this went on. The miller carried on being lazy and good for nothing and his wife carried on doing all the work and nagging the miller.

One day the good-for-nothing miller went up to the room we now call Room One. This is where they used to store the sacks of malt. The floor in those days was just loose planks of wood laid down between the beams.

The miller went up and he took one of the planks away.

When his wife took a sack of malt up she put her foot down... on nothing and tumbled down to her death. 'Now I'll have a quiet life,' thought the wicked miller.

But he was wrong. From that day on he had no peace. His wife haunted him. Whenever he put something down, she moved it. Whenever he tried to sleep she woke him up.

He went mad. It looked as if the mill would go to ruin but as soon as he had given up and gone, something happened.

The mill started to shine. It was always clean and always tidy. Always tidy, always welcoming.

People say it's the ghost of the miller's wife still looking after the place, dusting and polishing and tidying. She's happy in her work now that the miller has gone. But of course that's just a story. No one really believes in ghosts...

Just then Martin came in from the kitchen.

'OK,' he said. 'Who's the joker? Who's been in my room and tidied all my stuff away?'

7

The ghost trap

Everyone decided it was probably Marge or Joe who had tidied up but Katie was not so sure. Martin was not sure either. 'My things weren't just tidied up,' he said,

... they were POLISHED! And there was that funny smell in the air, you know...

Malt!

'I say we should do a bit of ghost hunting,' Martin said.

'Ooh,' said Katie, nervously.
'Do you really think we should?'
'I really think
we should,'
said Martin.

And so they did.

That night, Katie tried to stay awake. On her first night in the mill she couldn't get to sleep. Now it was her second night, she couldn't stay awake. The coo-oo-oo of the pigeons seemed soothing tonight. The gurglings and gigglings sounded friendly. The squeakings and creakings were comforting.

'Fancy being scared by that!' Katie thought to herself. 'It's only...'

And then there was a terrible
CRASH!
and a CLATTER and worse still an eerie

Everyone was awake now. And everybody was running towards the noise.

'What! What was that?'

Katie saw Martin running towards the noise. He had his camera.

'Quick! Hurry!' he shouted.

He pushed the door open and what did everyone see?

Miss Jackson, tangled in string, rubbing her ankles and howling, 'What IDIOT did this?'

Now Katie felt really scared.

It took a long time to explain. It took even longer for Miss Jackson to forgive them.

'It's just so stupid!' she said. 'THERE IS NO SUCH THING AS A GHOST!'

Katie and Martin hung their heads.

The other kids giggled. Martin felt silly.

'Fancy believing in ghosts,' he thought and blushed. He hated blushing. His face was so red now that his ears seemed to be glowing.

'Beetroot,' someone sniggered. Martin wished he were somewhere else. Anywhere else. He looked beyond Miss Jackson to the window. Suddenly his red ears went white. His face went white. He stood still and pale. He pointed a shaking hand towards the window.

Miss Jackson turned round. Behind her, in the pitch dark garden and reaching towards the window, a white figure flapped. It stretched its arm towards Miss Jackson.

'Fancy being frightened by a shirt on the washing line,' said Marge.

It was Miss Jackson's turn to go red.

Don't feel bad, Miss.

'It did LOOK like a ghost,' said Katie.

'I think the best thing we can do is forget all about ghosts,' said Miss Jackson. 'We need some sleep and we need to remind ourselves... What do we need to remind ourselves?'

'THERE IS NO SUCH THING AS A GHOST!' everyone chanted.

Then one by one they went back to bed.

8

A smell of malt in the air

The next day was their last day at the mill.

'I'm pleased with you,' said Miss Jackson. 'You've all tried lots of new activities. You've found out about the history of this area and this house and I can see you've all made lots of notes that we can use when we get back to school.

'And I think you've learned something else.' She looked at Katie. 'What have we learned?'

'There is no such thing as a ghost,' Katie sighed.

'Good!' said Miss Jackson. 'Now we've got time for a few games. Then we have to pack and tidy up. Some of us have got a lot to tidy up – haven't we, Martin?'

Martin blushed.

'Never mind for the moment,' said Miss Jackson. 'Just leave everything where it is and come out to the garden.'

Everybody trooped out to the garden. Marge went too.

So it was a surprise when everybody came back in to find… every piece of paper had been piled up.

Every pencil shaving had been swept up.

Every coat had been hung up.

Everything was neat and tidy.

And there was the smell of malt in the air.

About the author

I really do go with groups of children to stay in an old mill like the one in this story. I run writing courses there.

The mill really is supposed to be haunted. We really did work in chilly Room One and there *really* was a thunder storm! We all wrote poems and descriptions inspired by it. The poem on page 25 was written by one of the children on the course.